Twenty Steps to Wisdom

Jennifer James, Ph. D.

TWENTY
STEPS
TO
WISDOM

Newmarket Press *New York*

FIRST EDITION
97 98 99 10 9 8 7 6 5 4 3 2 1

LIBRARY OF CONGRESS CATALOGING-IN-PUBLICATION DATA
James, Jennifer, 1943-
    Twenty steps to wisdom / Jennifer James.
        p. cm.
    Based in part on expanded sections of the book Visions
from the heart.
    ISBN 1055704-302-7
    1. Conduct of life. 2. Self-realization. I. James, Jennifer, 1943-
Visions from the heart. II. Title.
    BF637.C5J35   1997
    158'. 1—dc2097-46529   CIP

AUTHOR SPEAKING ENGAGEMENTS
For information regarding speaking engagements by Jennifer James, contact
the author at P.O. Box 337, Seahurst, Washington 98062, or through e-mail
at jjanthro@msn.com.

QUANTITY PURCHASES
Companies, professional groups, clubs, and other organizations may qualify
for special terms when ordering quantities of this title. For information,
write Special Sales, Newmarket Press, 18 East 48th Street, New York, New
York 10017, or call (212) 832-3575.

Other Newmarket Titles by Jennifer James: *Success Is the Quality of Your
Journey, Windows, Visions from the Heart, Defending Yourself Against Criticism*

CONTENTS

Introduction	1
1. Awakening to the Need	9
2. Challenging the Present	15
3. Reaffirming Belief	23
4. Trusting in Self and Spirit	29
5. Clearing a Space	35
6. Elimination of Diversions	41
7. Commitment to Simplicity	45
8. Physical Balance	49
9. Feelings of Deep Rest	53
10. Balancing Rituals	57
11. Acceptance of Humility	61
12. State of Vulnerability	65

Contents

13. Clarifying the Mission   69

14. Choosing the Way   75

15. Finding the Feeling   83

16. Asking and Receiving   89

17. Translating   95

18. Checking the Fit   101

19. Making the Commitment   105

20. Transformation   109

    Bibliography   115

To Ted

INTRODUCTION

*Ignorance of spiritual laws is bondage; knowledge
of spiritual laws is freedom; application
of spiritual laws is wisdom.*

—Evelyn Underhill,
*Mysticism: A Study in the Nature and
Development of Man's Spiritual Consciousness*

THROUGHOUT TIME, individuals with heart and passion have sought greater power, intimate connection with the universe, and a sense of their own destiny. They seek to map their inner space, to move beyond the limits of their culture or religion, to know those things that cannot be known through intellect alone. They have an intense motive because they have a longing to increase their consciousness. They desire clarity in an increasingly complex and alienating world.

Introduction

When they are successful, they become "seed persons," those who change the nature of us all. They are enlightened. Many of the names of such seed persons are familiar: Krishna, Buddha, Jesus of Nazareth, Saint Paul, Mohammed, Dante, William Blake, Walt Whitman, Madame Guyon, Francis Bacon, Albert Einstein, Mohandas Gandhi, Aldous Huxley, Krishnamurti, Meher Baba, Gurdjieff, the Dalai Lama, Nelson Mandela. Add your own to this list.

We recognize the importance of visionaries. We want to know what they know, to be what they are. We believe they have access to paradise. Wisdom, in the form of enlightenment, is visceral and passionate, it is an ecstatic state. Many have described it as:

Enlightenment is a sensory and an emotional experience, an intellectual illumination, the feeling of being immersed in a flame, a sense of immortality, amazing grace, knowledge of the whole cosmic consciousness, the end of separations, your energy and intelligence are freed, life becomes simple, joy, radical understanding, inner wonders, love and peace, highest happiness, the ordinary becomes extraordinary, caught up into paradise, moral elevation, awakening, charisma, astonishing moments of insight, emotional ecstasy, an almost unbearable love for the world, lightness, intense relief, sensation of light penetrating everything, a feeling of the presence of God.

Such inner experience was once thought to be beyond our potential, limited to a single specialist within a community: a shaman, a guru, a priest, or a physician, who provided the community's channel between higher and lower powers. The "peasants" were excluded, as unaware or unworthy. They would always need intermediaries or translators. They could never be close enough to the power of God.

Most Americans are raised in traditions that put officials between them and their god. I call them wisdom bureaucracies. The only symbolic totem we are given at birth is a teddy bear or a purple dinosaur, and it is soon to be parked on a shelf. We are part of a sensible, rational culture that is only beginning to recognize native levels of memory, consciousness, and spiritual power. We give very little of "the spirit" to our children.

But we are ready to learn the wisdom path, the most powerful of all human gifts. We live in a time that invites all of us to seek deeper truths. It is the way out of the current chaos. It is a way to combine personal happiness with care of the community.

Much of our culture has been based on the belief that reality can only be known through empirical and quantitative science, but the path of spiritual concentration can also grant wisdom. The path of insight offers knowledge more likely to heal us. The intensity of this knowledge quest, for each of us, will either increase with age as life experience enhances trust of our own intuition, or wane as we stop believing that all things are possible.

BEGINNING THE JOURNEY

Wisdom is our collective learning through the ages. It is the accumulation and synthesis of our shared unconscious. It is what we all know deep down is right or true. Wisdom is the art of knowing or seeing things that are seemingly unknown or invisible, things that may only exist in the deepest places within the memory.

You can turn to any of the world's great wisdom traditions because they all share the same steps and the same path. There may be modern day interpreters who foment conflict between religions, but there are far more similarities between religions than differences. You can turn to any of the great philosophers or scientists, and despite the differences in various cultural and religious backgrounds, you will find that what wisdom seekers experience during their vision journeys is remarkably similar.

The twenty steps common to the wisdom traditions all create the same state of heightened awareness. These steps represent the known process, the known ways of opening yourself to a wider and deeper reality. These steps will take you beyond the common categories of the human mind and culture. There are many styles, and you will have many choices, but the basic path will remain the same.

All the wisdom traditions provide safety, reassurance, and direction. The only essential that you must have is your commitment to the power of understanding, and a rock solid belief in the truth of what lies within your heart and mind. You must trust the experience of your intuitive gifts.

You may prefer to join a group that explores these steps and prepares people for vision quests. You may want to seek a personal guide through your own school or church. Joseph Campbell, one of the great scholars and writers on myth and vision, said it is important to have a teacher because "some drown in the water that others easily swim in."

Most of us like to start out with armchair journeys rather than real ones, and that is a choice that this book easily fits. You can curl up now in a comfortable place and just play around with your mind's responses to the possibilities raised by the wisdom steps.

The Steps

Awakening to the Need

There is always a temptation to cover the abyss
with a trance.

—Marion Woodman,
The Pregnant Virgin

THE FIRST STEP is always the question, an opening within your heart and mind. It may feel like a small window that appears to show you a better way to do something or to think about something. You have an experience, you are somehow touched, there is a shift in your body and your awareness. Energy seems to flow into you, and you feel a unique connection with life. It can be anything from a small creative breakthrough to a major philosophical shift.

A man wrote to me recently describing his "awakening":

A few years ago I experienced something which is very difficult to describe. A "happening" that was, in part, a sensation, but mostly a mental awareness, or perhaps a brief glimpse, of the knowledge and understanding of all things.

It happened as I was walking in my backyard, and lasted only a few seconds, if that. My attention was drawn upward, and to the left, but I neither saw nor heard a thing. I stopped dead in my tracks, and to this day am not sure whether or not it was involuntary. I remember that my eyes were wide open and unblinking, and I experienced an effervescent sensation in the area above or around my head. It was as if a window in an invisible barrier had been opened for a brief moment, and at that time I had the knowledge of all things.

Many things can trigger these moments: the birth of a child, sunrise, sunset, the sound of the ocean, the smell of a forest, telepathic experiences, clairvoyance, immersion in music, dance, art, a garden, the power of a cathedral, near-death experiences, grief, falling in love, orgasm. All of them are ecstatic experiences that have been shared and imprinted through many generations.

The stories of other lives can transform us. Books can connect us with new sources of energy. Traveling creates an opening. Margaret Mead once provided her list of ways to achieve enlightenment: Study children (they are natural visionaries), study animals (our native selves), study other cultures (to learn universal truths), recover from a health or other life-threatening crisis, recover from a mental illness, or try a love affair with an old Russian.

Think back over your own moments of heightened awareness when a window to the world opened: One day, on a fishing boat traveling to Alaska through the majesty of the fjords, your consciousness changed; one week in another country loosened your sense of right or wrong; a chance to sleep deeply resolved a problem, a dream provided understanding.

An awakening may have come through the resolution of childhood pain when you recovered your true self. You realized how much you had given up long ago, and you began to reclaim it. We are often transformed in ways we feel but cannot name.

All of the wisdom traditions, including Christianity, describe such moments of enlightenment and encourage us to seek them. *Satori*, *nirvana*, *ecstasy*, and *ascension* are all described as the loss of self in the feeling of oneness, the end to separation.

As I write this I am listening to the voice of Beverly Sills; the beauty brings tears to my eyes, and passion fills the room. There are so many ways to awaken. We open at different times and in different ways. It matters not how, just that you are here, you have heard, you cannot stop. You have heard the call. It is the call to value your own life so you will value all life.

You may choose to deny what you feel. You may prefer to build a safe life within the compound of your own home, class or community, or you may choose to leave the limits of familiarity. If you have heard the call, then you must act. If you have never heard it, perhaps nothing is lost. If you hear it and ignore it, your life is lost.

Try to listen, to track the windows that open for you. Try to trace your awakenings. Notice the moments when your understanding seems to take a leap. What do you think is drawing you to ask deeper and more difficult questions about your life and your community? You are not alone.

We all have the ability to create this future story. We all have the potential, however latent, to be wise. To fulfill this potential there are guides, timeless rules. There are prerequisites, which thousands of years of experience have shown to be important. You were born with the memories, the internal knowledge of the wisdom traditions, but you must learn to access them.

With this first step, awakening to the need, you have begun.

STEP TWO

Challenging the Present

The fact is that the mad rush of the last 100 years has left us out of breath. We have had no time to swallow our spittle. We know that the automated machine is here to liberate us and show us the way back to Eden; that it will do for us what no revolution, no doctrine, no prayer, and no promise could do. But we do not know that we have arrived. We stand there panting, caked with sweat and dust afraid to realize that the seventh day of the second creation is here, and the ultimate sabbath is spread out before us....

—Eric Hoffer, *The Temper of Our Times*

AT CERTAIN POINTS in our lives, sometimes in times of crisis, we decide to challenge the present. Many cultures have rites of passage or initiation in which you are expected to question yourself and your reality. There are certain changes in a life that require information, guidance, ritual, and support. We need a boost to the next phase or stage. We need validation of what is happening.

We have few initiation rituals left in Western culture, and most of us need more thoughtful transitions from one age to another. We are beginning to treat midlife passage as one of these special times of review. It is considered a time to look at the first half of your life in order to decide what you will value for the last half.

The Plains Indians used a vision quest as a mark of the movement from boy to warrior. During the process you were expected to stretch your senses into another world, to gain the strength of a totem animal. You were then invincible and would be safe in battle. A young man went into the hills alone for many days. He might deny himself food and water until his *familiar* came. He might sacrifice a finger joint if all else failed; pain has always been a powerful teacher.

After successfully seeing or hearing his *spirit ani-*

mal, he would return home with a special song to be sung in times of fear, or to be used as a symbol of his communion and lifetime linkage with his totem. Many Native American names are drawn from the first vision experiences of childhood.

A male who could not achieve a successful warrior initiation might spend his life as a *berdache*, a male dressed as a female. These "specialists" took an alternative, a more philosophical or spiritual path.

The berdache was thought to have special powers because he had both male power and female intuition. The medicine man and the berdache were the tribal specialists in the pursuit of wisdom. They taught their people how to pursue higher and deeper awareness. There is a thin line between the dress and celibacy of modern day priests and the berdache; they are both gender-free guides.

Many cultures no longer teach the history, the variety of experience, the skills of the vision quest, so generations grow up without an understanding of the stirrings they feel at different times in their lives. We make up names for the obvious passages: baptism, confirmation, adolescence, menarche, birthday, first Holy Communion, Bar Mitzvah, quinceanera, menopause, retirement. But we do not clarify their impact.

Most of us notice when a birthday or crisis jolts us into questioning our existing environment or our current reality. A perceived failure might create instability somewhere in our lives. The balance has been disrupted, the harmony of whatever plateau we had previously reached is lost. Divorce, work problems, illness, or other losses shake up our routine.

Such divine discontent (think of them as tweaks from the gods) creates anxiety, perhaps depression, grief, or illness, and we realize we must reexamine what we thought was under control.

All of us get strong signals when it is time to do personal homework. You may be ill or less resistant to illness, losing sleep, tired all the time, seeing a counselor, tense, examining a new religion, going to a class, or joining some new leader you think might have the answers.

If you know what your questions are, write them

down. If you cannot identify your questions, it is time to ask yourself about the content and quality of your life to ascertain the level of challenge or discontent you really feel.

Go through your weekly and monthly schedule and highlight in your favorite color those activities that brought you some kind of pleasure or satisfaction. Highlight in a color that is not your favorite those activities you would rather not have done. Leave the neutral activities neutral. Even though many of us have to do things we don't like in order to pay our bills or be good citizens, you should be able to see, in color, what kind of negative and positive balance you have in your schedule. What are you willing to change?

Create a circle and divide it into three sections: individual, life work, and relationships. How does your time and energy get divided up in this pie? There is no reason for the wedges to be equal. If you are starting a new job, the life work wedge may be the largest. If you are ill, the individual wedge will be important while you concentrate on getting better. If you are raising small children, your relationship section will be the largest. Within the sections you can create as many subdivisions as you like:

❧INDIVIDUAL: physical, intellectual, emotional, spiritual.

❧LIFE WORK: paid work, creative work, community work, home maintenance, recreation.

❧RELATIONSHIPS: family, relatives, friends, colleagues, neighbors, support professionals.

Counselor Alene Moris describes the pie diagram, and its various wedges, as a *balance wheel* of your life that you can use to ask questions about what you are actually doing. You can see how you are spending your time and energy. You can compensate for perceived imbalance among the sections of the circle by knowing you are doing what you prefer. We all have self-selected strengths and weaknesses. Loving your work can take you through some lonely times. Friends can help you when your career falls apart.

CHALLENGING THE PRESENT

Most wisdom specialists agree that happiness can be described as 1) a belief that you control your own destiny, 2) an openness to new ideas, 3) a history of experiencing awakenings, and 4) seeing meaning beyond yourself. Ask yourself about your state of happiness. Do you control your own life? Are you open to new ideas? Have you, throughout your life, had moments of extraordinary awareness? Do you have deep connections to the world?

Ask yourself, Why am I doing what I'm doing? Does it bring me satisfaction or passion? Is it enough? What are my alternatives? Can you list five alternative ways of making a living, five places in which you could live outside of the region you now live in, five sources of love and support other than the individuals or groups you now rely on? How safe do you feel? What have been your biggest mistakes? What would you change if you had only a year to live? Do you know what you truly want?

Most of us are social animals, and that can be a source of great pain and energy loss. Imagine others discussing you, thinking you cannot hear them. What would you like to overhear them saying about you? What do you want to be able to believe about yourself? How has this changed over time? What is truly important to you? What has *heart* for you? What is the one thing that you are doing that will have impact beyond your life?

There are many ways to challenge the present, and it is often an automatic process. Start asking more questions and listening to the responses in your body. Slow down your external life during this journey, simplify as much as possible. The answers to your questions travel slowly, and sometimes the questions take even longer. They must be able to catch up with you.

Challenging the present takes you into a future chosen by you, unique to you. Scout the terrain of your life. We move forward by going deeper.

Reaffirming Belief

The hungry psyche has replaced the empty belly.
—Robert Ardrey

I AM OFTEN ASKED, by those who shun or ridicule self-knowledge, why people can be so preoccupied with understanding and changing their lives and selves. I answer that we, as a culture, are hungry for passion. We are hungry for a more intense connection with our life force. We once filled this need with the search for food and shelter. We are no longer satisfied by just multiplying supplies and floor space. We are now freer to ask about the quality of our lives, so we do.

The questions we asked in the past centered on Will I have enough to eat? not Will I eat too much? Once the stomach is full, many more of us are drawn to the search for understanding. It is no longer enough to be successful; we want to feel successful. We want internal as well as external satisfaction.

There are so many barriers to awareness in our culture that you need to know what you are willing to let yourself have. If the pleasure of knowing the value and direction of your life intimidates you, then you will block out the emotions and the questions. Childhood pain is often the central barrier to adult joy.

Alice Miller writes of the separation from *genuine self* that occurs when a powerless child tries to find ways to survive in a family that is unsafe. Marion Woodman writes of the loss of the feminine heart in women as they compete in a male world. Robert Bly speaks of the loss of trust in the good power of men.

Sheldon Kopp reminds us, "You must plow the fields of your past so that you can plant your own crops." Do your homework. Read, talk, join a group, seek counseling or guidance. Know what you can about yourself, your masculinity, your femininity, your shadow side, so that you can trust your intuitive gifts.

Do a family history so that you can know your past. Separate what you were told about your relatives from how they actually behaved. Set up a family tree, and note the most memorable characteristics of each person you include. Check the messages of your family and your culture. This is the environment within which you were raised.

Negative family visions can be powerful barriers. Adult children of alcoholics carry a legacy of an unsafe world that requires control, perfectionism, vigilance, pessimism, and defense. The need to shield their vulnerability often eliminates the self-trust and trust of others essential to wisdom.

There are many family biases against intuition and self-knowledge. There are also biases against self-esteem and independence. Which perceptions and values that you hold are the products of socialization, and which have you chosen for yourself? Do you know what your personal priorities are and what you truly believe in?

Watch out for traps like the Theory of Retribution, the idea that the gods are not on your side but are, in fact, competitors. This theory suggests that one should fear and placate the powers in the universe because, like us, they may be jealous and territorial.

Retribution takes us back to our earliest cultural experiments with religion. Early humans sought explanations for weather, accidents, life, and death. Animism, the belief that all things have spirits, provided many explanations that science now provides for us. Each object or power in the universe was given a personality, a transference of what a man knew about himself. The gods had to be satisfied, as powerful men and women did, if the tribe were to be allowed to prosper.

The sun god, the fertility god, the rain god, and the spirits of game animals all had to be rewarded and treated with reverence. If you wanted something, you had to give up something. Give the gods 10 percent of your crop or a sacrificial lamb, heart, or virgin, and you could safely keep the rest. We made deals, and in our psyche some of us still think we have to. We feel that too much joy or passion will invite the displeasure of others or of God, so we are careful to limit ourselves and our pleasures. We hide our light, we say we are sorry, over and over.

There is great truth in the idea of exchange. We should give back what we take. We should be aware of the balance, the connectedness of our lives, and the life that surrounds us. But retribution promotes behaviors based on fear, not awareness.

Rigid religious systems hold that only the specialists can have enlightening experiences. Most religions are structured like traditional monarchies with the king or pope as wisdom incarnate and the peasants as children. A religion or a religious leader that reduces an individual's faith in himself is not enlightened. Such wisdom shrinks rather than expands the possibilities of the faithful.

Any rigid system of thought—political, scientific, psychological, economic, or philosophical—limits access to information and growth. It is, however, possible to value highly and believe in a structure but, at the same time, be open to new perceptions and thoughts.

Participation in a wisdom journey requires you to believe that the powers of the universe are not only on your side but also within you. You must feel deeply that passion is your genuine life force and ecstasy is your inheritance. You deserve all that you will allow yourself to feel. We give to others from the overflow within us, not the emptiness.

Trusting in Self and Spirit

*The human spirit is virtually indestructible, and its
ability to rise from the ashes remains as long as the
body draws breath.*

—Alice Miller,
Prisoners of Childhood

REVIEW YOUR responses to change and crisis. It is
very difficult to have confidence in the information
available in the natural universe unless you have confidence in yourself. Think back over your life and ask
yourself these questions: How open do you feel you
are to change? How able have you been to follow
your intuitive judgments? Are you good at deciding
what is safe and what is not safe for you? Are you

more likely to follow what is offered by a leader, or do you sift possibilities through your own experience and values? Look back over your life and decide how good you are at basic survival skills. How has life turned out for you?

The more you know about yourself, your strengths and weaknesses, the more you will be able to contribute to your community. The more clearly you establish your values, the more awareness you have of your own behavior, and the more able you are to understand others, the easier it becomes to affirm yourself on any personal journey.

The basis of self-knowledge is an awareness of what you believe to be your value in this world. Take each of the following questions, one a day, and roll them around in your mind: What do you think you deserve? Do you consider yourself to be a good person? How much joy can you feel comfortable with? Are you able to resist the demands of others when they don't correspond to your own rights and needs? How able are you to be generous with others out of your own sense of abundance? How well do you take care of your intellectual, emotional, spiritual, and physical selves?

When you have faced crisis, trauma, or tragedy, how have you fared? Would you describe yourself as a survivor? Are you usually optimistic, confident, and independent? How well do you recover from disappointment, injustice, unexpected events, or changes precipitated by the decisions of others?

Can you travel long distances or in other cultures alone and feel secure? Have you hiked or spent time in a cabin or tent isolated from others? Would you do it again? Can you stand up for your beliefs when a group of your peers finds it unacceptable? What have you been able to do by yourself throughout your life? What is easy for you to do alone? What is hard? Do you need a witness to an emotional insight or a sunset to validate your pleasure and understanding?

Review any spontaneous experiences you have had (unexpected knowing, telepathy, insight, intuition, altered consciousness, communion with nature or another person, powerful connections to music, art, the world, the Spirit, a sense of harmony, a moment of compassion). Have you had passionate, visceral, opening events in your life? Were you able to accept the feelings of vulnerability that accompanied them?

Decide what kinds of preparation will strengthen both your ability to be open and your self-discipline. Talk to friends, teachers, or the spiritual guides you trust. Read in your areas of special interest. Eugene Gendlin's book *Focusing* provides a specific series of exercises to help you build trust in your intuitive spirit. The bibliography has a short list of helpful books.

Look at the religious and intellectual traditions you are part of and see what information and paths are offered. Watch out for limits. Religions and academics tend to name things; wise men and women rarely do. Scientists set up hierarchies and exclusionary language to separate the knowing from the unknowing. Arrogance generates ignorance, not wisdom.

This step is the longest you will face, but its length depends on the homework you have already completed. Age is on your side. If you are older or have faced many losses you will have answered these questions before. You will have often sought knowledge and guidance.

Most of us are experienced survivors in the mundane, practical, mortal world, but we have little experience with the sacred, spiritual, mystical, unusual world. We can feel the knowledge within us but have few skills for expanding it.

Many tribal cultures ascertain your readiness for a vision journey by measuring your experience and your faith. A tribal elder assigns special tests of endurance and skill. You can seek a leader or guide to devise tests for you, and ask him or her to grant you permission to continue along the path.

You can turn to counselors for support and clarification. But only you can decide what kind of journey you want to take and under what circumstances. The most important test is that you feel safe talking to yourself on a deeper level.

Here are some tests of inner strength:

- Go back into the past and make an apology
  for a mistake you made.

- Invite an enemy to lunch; you two have a lot in common.
- Confront a fear of an animal or an insect, a place, an activity, a memory.
- Write a letter to a dead parent or relative, and free yourself.
- Form an unusual friendship and learn from someone you once might have shunned.
- Give more than you want to for a cause you believe in, then come to terms with the conflict you feel.
- Speak up in public, gently, against an injustice. Repeat your statement until it is easy to say.

Wisdom paths are tests. They require a connection with self and the courage to follow the truth within you. There is no passion or vision in being someone else.

STEP FIVE

Clearing a Space

*When you get to be older and the concerns of the day
have all been attended to and you turn to the inner life...
well, if you don't know where it is, you'll be sorry.*

—Joseph Campbell,
The Power of Myth

THE CURRENT environment around us, the media in
particular, has created a giant conditioning mechanism
that both speeds up our thought and limits its depth.
We lose our imagination as electronic images flood our
senses. Touch, feeling, smelling, hearing, and deeper
memory are lost in the din. We cannot access the
knowledge we have in our bones, and our consciousness begins to atrophy.

In the 1960s some took drugs, as cultures have in religious and ecstatic rituals from the earliest times, to access deeper knowledge. LSD, for example, returns the user to a more mammalian state of awareness. It reverses the conditioning, the filters, of modern life; it restores more basic memories. On an "acid trip" one can observe and feel the relationship of all things.

Drugs may sometimes provide a rapid trip to heightened awareness but it is fleeting and too often destructive. The wisdom process we are engaged in here recognizes that there is no fast or secret formula for awareness, only time and intent. The real thing is always more difficult to achieve than the imitation.

Where can we find the space to think and feel? My work requires many airplane trips, and travel in the clouds is, for me, time to think. A seatmate once said to me, "Success is being able to go to your own home and feel comfortable." He had gone through a divorce and a job change. He had found that money and status offered few comforts when his family was disintegrating. Now he builds his life around his home so that, at the end of even the busiest work day, he knows where he most wants to be.

Home may provide time for renewal if you have a place to call your own, and you are at peace. But you must decide. The twenty-four-hour day has eliminated the once natural end of a day, so we must now create one. We need time, space, and an environment to be able to see that things are in balance, or to imagine a different path.

Some Basque communities take a child at age four to a sacred place, close by, and leave him or her alone all night to make a first contact with the world as a separate individual. It is a place the child has visited many times in the daylight with his or her parents. It is thought that each person must, early in life, make a personal contact with God.

When the children are fourteen they go to a hut in the mountains to stay alone for six months and solidify their connections to the earth and the Spirit. Usually they see no one, but in some cases there is another adolescent in a hut within walking range. The child chosen for the other hut is usually the one whom you liked least as you were growing up.

Most people do not find it easy to go on mystical journeys while in a common place. Religions have always created inspiring places, temples, or used drugs like peyote that create a separation from regular time and space. The hardest step in most quests is deciding to take the time. Being too busy is one of the ways we keep intuitive information at bay.

American culture has few traditions for clearing a space. Many other societies have formal requirements for life review. Every seven to ten years, they expect you to think deeply about your life and make changes. Many cultures believe that time spent in solitude is the most valuable time of one's life.

Clearing space for the information of the heart or the power of nature requires severance from other activities that we lean on for security and self-worth. It feels like a deprivation when we go into a different environment alone, until we adjust, or unless we welcome the change.

There are well-known elements that contribute to

the clearing of a space within your mind. There are many books and classes on meditation. Those practiced at meditations or vision journeys may be able to create the same environment, in their own home, that others must seek in the mountains.

Most wisdom traditions state that you must go outside. They believe that environmental beauty is essential to clearing a space because it reminds you quickly of the power of nature, the harmony, the natural order of things. Whether you are walking beside the ocean and feeling the centuries of tides or sitting in the shadows deep in a virgin forest, you can feel the forces that surround you.

All agree that solitude is vital to this experience. You must learn to feel safe alone. The presence of anyone else, particularly someone you know, will prevent you from being able to relax into yourself, your own values, and your intuitive center. The time alone you will allow yourself, to think about what you value, is a measure of the depth of your character.

STEP SIX

Elimination of Diversions

The work of preservation demands that the feelings
playing about in one's guts not be turned into action.
Just watch their passing like cherry blossoms.

—Maxine Hong Kingston,
The Tripmaster Monkey

IT IS TIME to resist any diversions claiming your attention so that there is room for something new. Settle yourself in all the ways you think might interfere with your concentration before you leave the known and predictable path. Carry a tablet or notebook around with you for a few days and write down everything that is worrying you. The list can include short-term, long-term, or future worries. Sit down and create a solution or a place to park each of these worries so that they do not come up when you are working on deeper issues.

Sometimes a worry box works. Put each worry on a card. List various solutions you have tried and the current one you are using. When a worry thought comes up see if you can make a note of it and put it back in the box. You can schedule times to review your worry cards instead of allowing them to pop into your head on impulse.

When you decide to take a wisdom journey put the worry box away as a symbol of release until you return. There will always be time to worry. Start a list of needs for your time away and for anything you think might occur at home to interfere. Prepare for what you can. Ask a friend to check on your home, plants, and animals so you will feel at peace.

You can also make a comfort list of your friends, skills, resources, and alternatives. We are sometimes better at listing the negatives in our lives than the positives. Make a list of your assignments for the future as you now see them. It will be interesting to make a comparison when you have reviewed these lists on a deeper level.

I always leave a clean house, laundry done, bills mailed, notes written, or calls made whenever I travel, regardless of the reason. I feel safer when I have ordered what I can order. External order seems to give permission for internal disorder.

One of the reasons many cultures insist that you leave home and seek a non-ordinary reality for higher consciousness is so that you can let go of everyday concerns and tolerate disorder in your mind.

You will begin to feel the release from diversions once you start the trip away. Removing yourself from the noise and speed of everyday life by traveling to a remote, or at least a quieter, place creates transformation. The environment has tremendous power. Go where you are most deeply touched by nature.

Choose a place that allows you to let go of the "buzz" inside you. Without cars, telephones, media, crowds, and obligations, you will slow down automatically. You will begin to catch up with yourself.

STEP SEVEN

Commitment to Simplicity

*We must learn to let go as easily as we grasp or we will
find our hand full and our minds empty.*

—Leo Buscaglia

AMERICANS NOW JOKE about retail therapy. We go
shopping in the hopes of acquiring a little more safety,
but end up with just one more thing to store. We wake
up tense on Saturday morning because we have so
much *stuff* that needs new parts, or cleaning, or repair-
ing, or using. Somehow having is not being. We are
hungry for passion yet we fritter away our lives with
details.

45

The wisdom path requires simplicity, at least for a time, so that you are free to think and not do. Wisdom travels much slower and offers a much quieter beat than the lives many of us have chosen.

Passion requires that you be unencumbered. Try to keep all your arrangements as simple as possible. Take less with you rather than more unless you need extra books, machines, and clothing to feel safe. Bareness will drive you inward. If you have ever trekked with your complete survival needs on your back, then you know the pleasure of carrying only the essentials. It is a feeling of freedom and balance.

There is no need to suffer—that will distract you too. Be prepared and safe. Simplicity limits the distractions of house, clothing, food, and equipment. Solitude reduces the other distractions. Try to clear your mind of things that you might use to divert yourself.

Once you are settled, begin to let go. Relaxing is an art that few of us have mastered. There are many techniques to help you learn. Use the ones that work for you. I find just creating a simple order with the few things I have brought with me works. It is like setting up an imaginary hut even if I am sitting on a beach. Do whatever you can to let go of the everyday until you are ready to stop fussing.

Try to leave on your journey with the things of the *small* mind taken care of so you can allow the big mind space.

The elimination of the distractions of modern life, the return to simplicity, will produce moments of guilelessness about the world, moments of feeling loved as a life (and no more) that will resonate throughout your body.

Physical Balance

Sometimes as I have sat in the audience watching Martha Graham dance, it has seemed to me as if she were unwrapping our body image which has been tied up for so long with the barbed wires of fear and guilt and ignorance and offering it back to us: a thing of honor.

Freeing at last, our concept of Self, saying to us, the body is not a thing of danger, it is a fine instrument that can express not only today's feeling and activities, but subtle, archaic experiences, memories which words are too young in human affairs to know the meaning of.

—Lillian Smith, *The Journey*

WISDOM REQUIRES both the body and the mind. The ability to feel or hear the intelligence of your physical body and its memories is a very important source of knowledge.

Eugene Gendlin describes the body as a "biological computer generating these enormous collections of data and delivering them to you instantaneously when you call them up or when they are called up by some external event."

We all have physical auras or collections of physical impressions, although it is difficult to sense our own. We usually can quickly pick up the aura of another person. We can read their signals of safety or danger.

But we are so good at concealing our own being from ourselves that we do not even realize that others may know things about us that we do not. Counselors often act as mirrors for their clients. When our defenses break down because we allow them to, through choice, relaxation, grief, or exhaustion, we can see more clearly.

The marathon encounter groups of the 1960s used exhaustion to break through the defenses of participants. Many traditional and mythological quests require that both body and mind be extended to their utmost limits. The same breakthrough to new perceptions can be achieved through acceptance and love of your body.

One way to reach acceptance is through physical balance. Find the most comfortable sense that you can within your own physical being. Your body will become a distraction if it is not comfortable. You know what works best for you, but most journeys start with a cleansing and soothing of the body as well as the mind. Many tribes and clans use special scents, bathing, music, and colors to create balance and as a signal to the gods that they are ready.

Clean everything you want to. Clip, cut, rearrange until you feel ready. Wear clothing made of natural fibers that are loose and provide no maintenance problems. That is why gurus always seem to prefer flowing robes. They are just more comfortable for lounging around.

Many traditions cleanse the body internally as well, with fasting, sweat baths, aromas, purifiers, special emetics, or herb mixtures. You can take care of your food needs in any simple way but it seems important to exclude alcohol, coffee, overly processed foods, sugars, and any mind-altering substances. Review your basic needs so that your body can cooperate, and concentrate on feeling, instead of food or temperature.

Acceptance of the body requires a further step. Many addicts or anxious eaters are trying to fill a void within. They may create such barriers that they cannot even feel, let alone accept, their bodies. The emptiness does not always show but they know it is there.

It may help to do an inventory of what you like and don't like about your physical body. Ask yourself what you are willing to change and what you will probably not change. Make your peace with whatever it is you don't like. Your body does not have to be a monument to the pain, problems, or negatives that you have collected.

Let your body be free, at least for this time. You can always go back to the cramped positions later. Take a deep breath, put the negative aside, stretch, shake loose, welcome your body. Take all of you to the next step.

STEP NINE

Feelings of Deep Rest

We can make our minds so like still water that beings gather about us that they may see, it may be, their own images, and so live for a moment with a clearer, perhaps ever with a fiercer life because of our quiet.

—W. B. Yeats

WE MOVE SO FAST in American culture that few of us remember the feeling of deep rest. We are attracted to advertisements showing women who seem to be serenely resting in hot tubs or waking from a perfect night's sleep on a new mattress. We can rarely remember actually doing that ourselves. We may buy the hot tub or the mattress but never acquire the feelings of rest that attracted us in the first place.

Many of us are so out of touch with our bodies that we deny them the basic need to rest. We pride ourselves on a discipline that gets more than it should out of us. Some of us see rest as wasted time rather than as a source of energy and renewal.

Do you remember those special times on a vacation, or when you have slept in, and your mind and body feel just right? The body knows when it is ready to awaken, if we do not override it with our demands. Deep rest occurs when you can set down the burdens of your day or life and feel the freedom of a new start. It is very hard to look at all that you carry unless you set it down.

There are many activities that help us eliminate distractions and achieve rest. Certain things create an experience of letting go. Some feel this way when swimming. They are creatures of the water and have always known it. Swimming laps or just being submerged in water gives them a feeling of deep rest. Exercise breaks down patterns of tension for others, and dancing, running, stretching, and aerobics work well.

Massage can be a wonderful source of deep rest because the laying on of hands is so healing. You are turning your body over to another person, whom you trust, to treat it gently and return it to you. Yoga can produce the same deep rest as therapeutic massage. Sitting quietly while you dream, staring into space, or emptying your mind can create a feeling of peace.

It is a challenge to see how long you can sit with comfort and do nothing. Many of us have to learn to sit still, to relax, and let our minds clear. That is why Americans pay for meditation classes. It does not seem to be a skill that we grow up with.

Deep breathing is probably the most powerful source of a state of rest. The body needs air for life, but most of our breathing is shallow and quick, whereas the lungs thrive on longer, deeper breaths.

I find sleep to be a wonderful restorer of spirit. Rearrange your schedule to allow yourself enough sleep and a gentle awakening. Refuse to participate in activities that deny you rest. When time allows, let your body sleep as long as it wants to, undisturbed by light or sound. Your body will respond to a nap if you create the environment: dark, quiet, safe, clean.

A vision journey requires the best of what you have physically, which is the body's most natural state.

STEP TEN

Balancing Rituals

*Breath is the bridge which connects life to consciousness,
which unites your body to your thoughts. Whenever your
mind becomes scattered, use your breath as the means to
take hold of your mind again.*

—Thich Nhat Hanh,
The Miracle of Mindfulness

MANY WISDOM TRADITIONS recognize how hard it is
to clear the mind, so they use special rituals—spinning
prayer wheels, rosaries, chanting, singing, dancing, Tai
Chi—all concentrate and clear the mind. Church cere-
monies, making circles of stone, the beautiful Hopi and
Tibetan sand paintings are all rituals of both respect
and concentration.

The smell of incense immediately takes me to
church, even if my eyes are closed. I was raised going

57

to one of those small, dark, mysterious-with-stained-glass Anglican churches. Any of the senses responds strongly to memory, and just triggering one of them can put you into the right frame of mind. Hymns resonate in the hearts of many of us. Candles, flames, light are powerful mediums.

Any symbol that centers the mind is useful. Wisdom traditions create a certain set of ritual movements or objects to signal memory and return us to reverent places in our minds. Hypnosis is a relaxation technique that can both open and concentrate the mind.

These tools are called "rites of intensification" by anthropologists. Some of these rites involve the whole group or community. Societies may hold rites of intensification to protect a village; to ensure rain, sun, or fertility; or to prepare the way for an individual undertaking a journey.

You may decide to hold a celebration for your friends and family before you start on your way. The power of our friends surrounding us and offering their help is not to be underestimated.

There are as many balancing rituals as there are communities. It is the unique nature of humans to keep inventing new ways to live. Some American snake handlers believe that picking up a venomous rattlesnake is a confrontation with the supernatural. Those free of sin will be cleansed. Those who are not free of sin will be bitten and die.

I was raised to believe that the symbolic consumption of the body and blood of Christ would restore my spirit. Confession, absolution, and symbolic consumption are common rituals in all religions. Religious objects of all sorts, including bones, robes, and other relics, have always been used to evoke powerful emotional responses.

Each of us has our own sense of what creates balance within. Jigsaw puzzles and gardening are wonderful concentration tools for me. Bonsai gardening or the tea ceremony are balancing rituals. What clears your mind and brings you to your center? You know the feeling of balance. What do you have to do now to achieve it?

Acceptance of Humility

*The most beautiful and most profound emotion we can ex-
perience is the sensation of the mystical. It is the sower of
the true science. He to whom this emotion is a stranger—
who can no longer stand wrapped in awe—is as good as
dead. That deeply emotional conviction of the presence of a
superior reasoning power which is revealed in the incom-
prehensible universe forms my idea of God.*

—Albert Einstein

ACCESS TO WISDOM, to the resources of a greater
power, requires that we recognize the limits of our
own. We must make a conscious choice to open ourselves to knowledge. Connection to a non-ordinary
reality, to the power of the supernatural, assumes
that you accept the existence of a power greater than
human.

Humility is not fear; it is an attitude. Each of us seeks wisdom, in a condition of poverty and need. We abandon, albeit briefly, the protection of our usual thoughts, frames, controls, and structure. Our minds, and therefore our souls, become defenseless.

Early religions often created ego-poverty through fasting, self-flagellation, self-mutilation, and prostration. Many Christian sects still believe you must approach God with your eyes cast down, on your knees, covered in sackcloth and ashes.

Suffering is thought to produce a heightened state of awareness. The ordeals or tests of a quest allow the breakthrough to special knowledge and the revealing of the sacred. The mind and heart may open in crisis, as we search for new solutions, in ways that they do not in our normal routine.

Sacrifice symbolized the willingness to offer a gift to the greater power in recognition of one's own position as a supplicant. Suffering is a form of sacrifice, but many cultures believe that the giving up of time, ego, or property is just as powerful. Given our current life-style and values, time may be a most appropriate sacrifice.

The Northwest Coast tribes understood the importance of humility. They required a private but complete confession of all the faults of the supplicant. Wisdom required the revealing of a genuine and honest self. The motivation for rituals of humility is not very different from that of the confession and purification rituals of contemporary churches.

Try to clear out your past by recognizing personal mistakes and errors. List those circumstances where you were unkind, harsh, or disrespectful of life. Assign an appropriate penance to yourself; there is no need to ask others. Make your apologies in whatever way you can; try to atone.

You can make a call, write a letter, send an anonymous gift, donate to a charity, accept an apology from someone else. If your regrets center on someone who is dead, find another way to atone. Give where you can now give, take care of another child or another relative.

A friend of mine who was once unfaithful to his wife washed her car every Saturday for a year. He provided her a visible penance that eased her pain and restored her trust. On the last Saturday she joined him and they washed the car together.

Admit your mistakes, forgive yourself and others. The frame of your mind is the most important condition of this journey. Wisdom will be available in direct proportion to the sincerity of the seeker.

State of Vulnerability

The soul does not like unconscious ecstasy.

—Robert Bly

WITH HUMILITY comes vulnerability; we admit our ignorance and our weakness. In the Christian traditions the prophecy "But the meek shall inherit the earth and delight themselves in the abundance of peace" (Psalms 37:11) refers not to a demeanor with one's fellow humans as much as a willingness to be vulnerable before both a greater power and the wonders of the world.

Inherit means, not the riches of the material life, but the richness of deep awareness. The world becomes ours because we can feel it, smell it, touch it, and love it. Heaven on earth is this reality and our awareness of it.

We all have a desire, a remarkable need to transcend ourselves, and many more of us are now free to do so. Skills that were once available only to "specialists" are more available to everyone.

We are far safer in our bodies and minds in this time than at any previous time. We are more at home in our psyches. We do not need to spend a lifetime experimenting to be able to converse with ourselves. We have been raised in a psychological age that creates the foundation for a voluntary step into the spiritual and natural realms.

Those who traveled long before us accepted the power of nature but rarely their own power. Opening to the unconscious, acknowledging self, was once discouraged as a sin. It was to be repressed except in the form of dreams. Dreams were thought to be the medium through which the gods sent messages to mortals.

We now have far more access to unconscious information and cultural permission to be adventurous with feelings. We do not need to hide so much from ourselves, others, and the gods. But that does leave us more alone. We are creating with our own substance rather than just following tradition.

Complete acceptance of your inherent vulnerability is the assignment at this step on the path. Increased consciousness, despite the feeling of vulnerability you may have, allows attention to sensory experience, the silences and sounds of the environment. Your sensitivity is the opening that makes you available to wisdom.

There is rapture in the meeting of the inner and outer worlds. As you sit alone, wherever you have chosen to be, prepared, available, the separate parts of yourself and your environment will begin to connect. It is a process of slowly becoming aware, becoming conscious of inner murmurings. A single connection or insight may not create a new understanding, but many small steps will start the focus toward one. When a single "happening" resonates, a path will begin to appear.

Clarifying the Mission

The task is to go as deeply as possible into the darkness, to name the pain that one finds there, and the truth of one's perceptions, and to emerge on the other side with permission to name one's reality from one's own point of view.

—Anthea Francine,
Envisioning Theology

IN SOME SOCIETIES, a spiritual leader will take you to this point of preparation and then leave you alone to carry out your mission. You may have known your mission when you decided to pick up this book. Illness, divorce, unemployment, loss, or change can clarify our priorities very quickly. You may want a deeper knowledge of what is happening to our culture, or our politics, or just increased understanding.

The questions are often the answers, but there are so many that you must set your priorities. Often answering the big ones settles the little ones. What do you want to know about yourself? What do you want to understand about the world you live in? What do you need to know about your work or your future?

You must know your motivation before you have a chance of success in your mission. If your motivation is negative, i.e. to harm someone, to get even, to compete or win, you are thinking of control, not understanding. Put those thoughts aside; they will be easy to pick up again later.

Some of us do not have specific questions or problems to solve. Our question might be very general. What is this about me? Is anything missing? What do I want? What is truly important to me? What do I want to be able to believe about myself? What is entering my life at this time? What is leaving my life? What is happening around me? What can I do to make a difference?

Choose any question that fits, that resonates or

seems to touch something within you. The following ideas will help you to proceed:

- Identify the life you really want.
- Imagine yourself achieving it. What does it look and feel like?
- Close your eyes and picture yourself in five years.
- What do you look like, what are you wearing, where are you, who are you with, how do you feel?
- Think about what you would have to do to get what you want.
- Recognize and list the barriers to what you want.
- What is the smallest step you could take toward this goal?
- What do you want to give to your community or the world?

An unknown or more open-ended mission can be

harder than this basic life review but consequently more rewarding. When you ask, "What is it about me?" you may get an answer that hurts or startles. When you ask, "What happened to my marriage?" you may find out that you were not willing to be intimate, that you were not truly available for marriage. Follow the most powerful question.

The most important wisdom journey I took had as its mission the question, What is this hole in my center, this missing part, that keeps me somehow detached from people? It had taken me so long just to realize it was there because I was so skilled at covering it up. I selected relationships that would not challenge the flaw.

A divorce finally forced me to ask this question on the deepest level of my being and not to give up until an answer resonated within me. This quest of mine was both general, What is going on? and specific, What has kept me cut off from intimacy?

The process of clarifying your mission can be very powerful because it represents and communicates your purpose: Here is what I stand for, here is what I believe, here is what I am committed to. The answers are always there. The key lies in one's ability to apprehend them, to be ready, to feel safe with what one learns.

You must be willing to allow your heart and mind to be touched. We are all called on this path to be our own unique selves. Only when our mission is clear can we see and support others.

Choosing the Way

*Heroes and heroines move out of the society that would
have protected them, and into the dark forest; into the
world of fire, of original experience. Original experience
has not been interpreted for you, and so you've got to work
out your life for yourself. Either you can take it or you
can't. You don't have to go far off the interpreted path to
find yourself in very difficult situations. The courage to
face the trials and to bring a whole new body of possibilities into the field of interpreted experience for other people
to experience—that is the hero's deed.*

—Joseph Campbell,
The Hero With a Thousand Faces

ONCE YOU HAVE chosen your mission, it is time to
review the journey and consider the way you prefer to
learn. Do you want to take the more common path
through to the light? It is a legitimate choice. Do you

want to take the deeper path to the darker sources of experience?

Many religions or philosophies emphasize light—sunrise services, candles, crystals, arms stretched upward, music, art, architecture. The spires of churches take us to heaven. The word "light" is a word of impact, of opening. The idea of breaking through to the light, becoming light, feeling the light within. It is an outward journey to create a oneness with the universe. It requires no special instructions. It is a familiar path.

You pitch your tent and wake before dawn, or you take a hike at sunrise. You welcome the first light and use it to inspire renewal. Candles at Christmas symbolize the light that takes us through the shortest, and therefore the darkest, days of the year. Crystals capture the light and bring it close to your being.

There are also wisdom traditions that require you to pass through the darkness to reach the light. Most of us have a natural resistance to the dark side, but the shadow is a very old theme in mythology and religion. Heroes had to travel through hell and confront monsters to obtain love or power. The Crucifixion is a horrible death leading to eternal life. The path of the martyr was usually one of torture. The Buddha left his home and placed himself at the mercy of passersby as a beggar. Nelson Mandela spent twenty-six years in prison.

When hallucinogenic drugs were used to seek enlightenment many people were afraid of dark visions. They panicked and ended up on bad trips. They were seeking pleasure and rejected the frightening information their minds presented. Tribes that used mind-altering drugs like mescaline sought understanding, not sensation. They expected intense experiences. Without preparation, the conflict between light and dark can seem like madness.

Shamanic journeys always use the darker paths to expand understanding. They do not require drugs, just deep relaxation or intensification rituals, and a willingness to release psychosocial defenses. Drums or chants are often an important part of the shamanic journey inward. They are images of going deep into the earth (or self), instead of upward and away from the earth. They are heavier, more fearsome images, and their power is great.

A shamanic journey is less familiar than a sunrise meditation in contemporary culture. These are the basic steps:

Put yourself in a darkened place, either outside at night, in a building or in a tent that light does not penetrate, or cover your eyes in some way. You may use drum rhythms to lull the body into a mood that facilitates the journey. Deep breathing may also help you relax and open.

Find within your mind an image of a hole in the earth, an entry point through which you can gain the illusion of access. It should be an actual hole in the environment (cave, crevasse, hollow tree, gopher hole, well) into which you can let your mind wander. Remember Alice in Wonderland tumbling down the rabbit hole?

At some point on your journey downward, through this hole that you visualize, look for a tunnel.

There may be many tunnels, or it may just seem like a big black space. There should be a feeling of heading downward until you feel you have entered what shamans call "the lower world."

Look around in your imagination and then return to the surface as an experiment in the illusion of coming and going. You need to feel comfortable with your ability to come and go when traveling in unfamiliar psychic territory.

When you feel rested and ready, use your mind to return to the tunnel and ask for an animal escort (mammal or bird). It must be a wild animal, because domesticated animals have lost their power. It cannot be a reptile, because they are not warm-blooded. An image of an animal or bird will appear. My spirit came in the form of an owl.

This animal becomes your totem or protector, and in many tribes was a lifetime source of power that might be incorporated into your name. The human/animal alliance recognizes the oneness of life forms. You probably have an affinity for an animal or bird now, with pictures on your wall, but have not seen it as a guide.

At this point you can begin your mission. Ask your questions and ask the animal to help. It may take more than one journey or symbolic animal in your consciousness to find an answer. Some animals will have power and, therefore, information for you; others may not. Any animal that seems threatening is to be avoided: gently pass by.

Once you have made contact with your totem or symbolic animal, many shamans report the feeling of encountering, in the darkness, a bridge that they must cross with the help of their "power animal." Only on the other side can they hear what the universe is trying to tell them. It is a bridge into "sacred space" or non-ordinary reality. If you feel uncomfortable during this imagined journey, always return to the surface and open your eyes.

Psychotherapy or counseling, in almost any form, can also be a journey into the dark. We haven't traditionally referred to analysis as a wisdom quest because we believe it is a rational process grounded in acceptable reality. Yet many therapists are actually using shamanic processes.

Anyone who has participated in analysis, as either healer or client, knows the truth of the peeling away of the layers of our behavior and understanding. The journey to *true self* is a painful quest of the most intimate kind. It is a way of passing through the tunnel, of being reborn into the light of self-acceptance.

You can choose any path, but in your lifetime there will be journeys filled with light and those that take you to darker realms within nature and your own mind. The light and the darkness are equal in their power, wisdom, and visionary capacity. You can choose what you believe will teach you what you need to know.

Consider your questions and their connection to you. Is this to be an external or an internal journey? This is highly personal territory. Let your sense of self and your sense of safety guide you.

Finding the Feeling

*Every bad feeling is potential energy toward a more
right way of being if you give it space to move
toward its rightness.*

—Eugene Gendlin,
Focusing

WHEN YOU PUT yourself in a special environment asking
for wisdom you will be flooded with information and
memories. You will remember long-ago hurts and joys.
You will find that genetic memories also surface. Carl
Jung described much of what we are as shared unconscious memories that have become a part of our DNA.

The subjects that your mind explores may surprise
you. Let it roam. Intuitive wisdom will bring up the

heart of a problem when your mundane self may be concentrating on something entirely different.

When you tire of freewheeling, review your agenda. Move within when you are at a place of calm and deep rest, and ask yourself about the quality of your life. How does it feel? What is most important to you at this time? What has brought you to this place? If there are too many questions, let them revolve freely in your mind and body until one or two take precedence and seem to carry more power or emotion.

It may help to center on a particular area of your life: family, self, profession, community, health, relationships, children, spirit. If no questions appear, or no single one seems particularly intense, just relax, breathe, and feel your body. A lack of information is almost always due to a block or tension within the body. When the body releases, the mind does.

Be gentle with yourself, take very small steps with the play of emotions until you make a visceral connection. If you are stuck, be patient. Try tapping into the *sense* of what you may now be feeling. Try to formulate it into a question. What shape, color, texture, smell does it have? The smell I was confronted with on one occasion was strong, the sweat of a working man. Smell triggers memories deeper than any of our other senses.

Choose one idea from those which you are considering. How does the question or problem physically feel? Can you get a sensory response from your body? Is there a tingle or a punch of recognition that this thought has power for you? Do tears begin to flow, or do you feel pleasure? Are you afraid, or is there anticipation?

Most questions or thoughts have more than one visceral element to them. One way to clarify a problem is to break it into parts and think about each part separately. What is most important is to maintain your intuition, the strong sense you will have of what fits and what does not.

Try at this point to name what you are feeling about the whole or a part of it. Try to name the emotion, and test the fit until it feels right. Does your question, feeling, or problem make you confused, tense, heavy, tired, excited, open, closed? What seems to be the worst part of it? What is the best? Can you give it a name and formulate a question?

Can you describe it? Is it big, little, light, dark, old, new? Your body knows, and it will tell you. As you experience these feelings or remember something that happened to you, are you younger, a child, your present age, older, scared or happy?

Once you know the feeling, ask, What would expand this feeling? What would change this feeling? How would I feel if I understood this problem or it was completely resolved? You need to know the quality and intensity of what you are trying to understand.

I had resolved to ask about the feeling that something was missing inside of me. It had led to unreasonable fear on more than one occasion. It was strongest whenever I tried to love and trust someone. I thought that this question contained my deepest secrets.

You may find your question is not personal but cultural. Why is there so much violence? Why do so many of our leaders seem unaware? Answers to questions about the world can often be found within the answers to our own problems.

Say out loud the word or words that come closest to describing what you feel, or write them down. Do they resonate within you? Often you will feel your stomach jump with a little spasm of pleasure or fear when the link is made. Any bodily signals, especially sexual ones, will affirm the power of your question. A body "shift" of any kind is the beginning of a transformation.

Receive whatever comes with an open mind; stay vulnerable. Sift information rather than quickly grabbing it. Gently clarify what you feel, and see if it is possible to put it into words.

Let the feeling move around in your body until you can name it. The name that eventually resonated deeply within my body was "abandonment." It was the word that turned up after "bad," "empty," "thin," "lost," "young," "dark," "old," "closed," "hole," "too late," "alone," "unloved," "unlovable," "afraid." When I asked about the problem of violence only one word appeared, "fear."

You may ask questions over days or hours, and you may receive answers in the same way. It is important to keep your heart open, to move slowly, to maintain your solitude, to be gentle with yourself until you feel the quest, for this moment in time, is complete. It will be obvious when it is finished. You will feel clear, energized, or you may just want to curl up and go to sleep.

STEP SIXTEEN

Asking and Receiving

The beads of knowledge are already accepted: it is only necessary to string them together into a necklace.

—Ken Wilber,
A Brief History of Everything

THE CORE OF a wisdom journey is the process of asking for information from the sources around you and being able to receive the answers. When you have found comfort with a way to reach within, choose just one of the feeling words you have discovered.

Reconsider it, roll it around in your mind and body, then stand back from it. If you are unable to form your thoughts into a question or word, then just ask again, What is this feeling? What does it mean for me, for my life? You will get many answers or only one. If you get many, some will be transitory and will produce no further visceral shift within you. Let them go by until you receive an answer, or information that produces a sense you can feel.

Imagine yourself as a wise person (pick your favorite: Solomon, Buddha, Jesus of Nazareth, Gandhi, Eleanor Roosevelt, Einstein) sitting in the center of the feeling or asking the question, What do I hear?

If you are outside, ask for help from the natural resources around you: the sky, the water, the trees, the animals. If you have chosen a shamanic journey, ask the darkness or your power animal. Each answer that fits will create a little or a big "wow" deep within. You will know. It is like an orgasm; there is no confusion when one has occurred. Receive whatever comes; stay vulnerable.

Consider the information that continues to flood your mind and body, rather than quickly accepting it. Probe the answers and repeat your questions. Try again to gently clarify what you feel and see if it is possible to put it into words. If you have decided to keep a journal, now may be the time to write down what you have learned.

You may continue to ask questions. It is important to keep your mind open, to maintain your solitude, until you are tired. It will be obvious when you are finished. You will find yourself slipping into neutral, wanting to walk or putter around while your mind and body process all you have felt and learned.

When I first took these steps, I had a very open agenda. What was this feeling inside that seemed to limit me in so many ways? The feelings around it were fear and pain. Eventually when the word "abandonment" formed out of these, it was a fit deep within me. I knew it was the truth.

Information came flooding in. As a small child, almost from birth, I had been left. I was born in London during World War II. I spent my first night and every night for three months in a bomb shelter. My parents were both police officers, and their duties during the war and the bombings took them away. It was a time of great fear. My brother and I were eventually sent out of the city, as many children were, to the safety of the countryside. I was moved often from relatives to foster homes to orphanages and to places my parents were assigned.

When my father, who had been a mine engineer before he became a policeman, was sent to work in the mines for three months to produce coal for the war effort, I went with him and was put into day care. I was only two, but the memories were there. I knew for the first time, when I took a wisdom journey, that as a very small child I had been abused in some way. I could smell the coal dust and sweat of the person who had hurt me. I also knew, clearly, that it had not been my father.

I had sought that smell out my whole life and never known why. Somehow that early hurt, whatever it was, sent me so far inside myself that only as a mature adult was I willing to begin to trust again. For the first time I was able to remember some of these experiences and accept their impact on my life.

One of the most telling images that surfaced was of a one- or two-year-old child lying in a small bed in a strange place, tucked in tight. I had the idea that if I could lie in the bed quietly enough, if I didn't move a muscle all night, I would still be there in the morning. As a child, later, when the family was reunited, I would still try to find a tight, dark place in my bed to create safety and the feeling of being held. I learned to go under the covers to the foot of the bed and wedge myself between the end of the mattress and the tucked-in bed clothes.

I was trying to figure out the rules for survival. There was some connection between the hurt, the fact that I was rarely held or touched, and the frequent abandonment. I was so young, and I needed to understand to know what was expected of me. This knowledge has led to a lifelong commitment to work for hurt children.

Your questions may not be so inwardly turned. You may have community, family, or work issues that you want to know more about. You may seek direction during a time of ambivalence. Sometimes what you receive fits your need, but often it can uncover another, deeper need. Whatever happens, you get to decide what to do next.

Where your pain is, you will find your soul. But change always produces a sense of loss, and the grief can be overwhelming. Be prepared: all of the wisdom traditions refer to this abyss, the bottomless pain. You must lean into the pain because the darkest moment holds the deepest truth.

Translating

*Profound joy of the heart is like a magnet that indicates
the path of life. One has to follow it, even though one
enters into a way full of difficulties.*

—Mother Teresa

ONCE THE INFORMATION and the direction is
yours, a new barrier is encountered. We resist using
what we know to be true. We resist change even when
our conscious mind knows it is required. We resist even
when it is written down. The unconscious resists giving
up long-held patterns. Perhaps it is hardest when we
resist forgiving. We find it as hard to forgive ourselves
as we do to forgive others. We want to reclaim the past
instead of taking from it what is good and moving on.

The process of translating what we have received can be the longest step to wisdom.

Once I had a word, "abandonment," and an answer, I was left aware but unsure. I could peer into the empty place but not fill it. I would wake at night in pain. The most unprotected time in our night, the hour before dawn, is called the "hour of the wolf" by some cultures. It is the hour when the self, still sleepy, confused, cannot defend itself against the thoughts that destroy our confidence. It is the hour, according to the legends, when the great Russian wolves catch and eat their prey.

But we learn on wisdom journeys that out of the darkness comes light. Creating alignment among your resources, energies, and thoughts requires conscious effort and an acceptance of this process. It is a choice you make. When you accept that these ancient steps are shared by many, you are not alone, the pain passes quickly.

My friend Max, a business consultant, learned about his life by foreseeing his death. This is his account:

Imagine yourself in the place I was nearly two years ago. The setting was the Mount Madonna

Retreat Center, outside of Santa Cruz. During the quiet of an afternoon's rest in my room, a strong inner voice jolted me out of my tranquil state. "Max, you have four years. What is the one thing you will do to have the greatest impact?" Without a moment's hesitation, I heard myself responding, To create as much magic as I possibly can.

I was shocked and confused. The reference to four years. What did that mean? The end of life? A new beginning? What do I know about magic, much less creating it?

A lot of thought has since gone into the message of that inner voice. I gathered information on magic. I reflected on what I had read and heard. I listened to that assured laserlike voice inside me. A kaleidoscope of thoughts flashed through my mind. Magic as life's splendid torch. Passion as a hunger deep in the cells of the body. What was the magic?

As a management consultant, I had helped organizations examine what they want to look like, feel like, and create for their futures. Organization leaders rarely demonstrated an inclination to embody the ideals and values implied in this type of strategic planning. They were not interested in the big picture.

I realized it was up to me to design a vision planning procedure that would empower them. I had to help them to know that people can create what they really want. I designed a vision planning program for businesses that would provide inspiration and energy. I knew what my contribution could be.

Max changed his life and his business. He became more successful at both. He could not change his destiny (a terminal illness was diagnosed shortly after his vision), which had been revealed to him on his retreat; he could only use it well.

The translating process allows the answers you feel to evolve into action. What do you want to do now that you have a handle on the problem or an answer to the question?

I decided I needed to learn how to trust and how to love. I had been an expert to others but not to myself. I sought counseling; I needed an experienced guide. We joked that I was truly learning the ABC's of love. I had always gone on form before; now I would let myself trust and feel the actual content of a relationship.

The counselor taught me to notice how I was treated and how others responded to the way I treated them. I learned about behavior, not words. I sought out friends who told the truth and were able to touch and be touched. I stayed away from people who had not come to terms with their own monsters.

I finally knew what my assignment was. I became able to transcend my perceived abandonment. I learned to face the normal conflicts in relationships instead of hiding from them. It was hard; other people's anger frightened me, but I persisted. My life changed. I am now able to love and be loved. I am no longer tightly tucked in. The empty place is growing smaller and smaller. The feeling of abandonment is almost gone.

The most startling change has been a loss of interest in my own personal problems. Something shifted within me that released more of my energy to the outside. I now work on social (children's issues and racism) and business problems. I decided that if business executives became more willing to lead with wisdom, all our lives would improve.

STEP EIGHTEEN

Checking the Fit

Fortunately, analysis is not the only way to resolve inner conflicts. Life itself still remains a very effective therapist.

—Karen Horney

ONCE THE WISDOM of the mind begins to surface, it needs to be checked against what we know about ourselves. Do our values, interests, talents, resources, and obligations support the answers we've received? Does the actual activity of your old life move in the same direction as your vision, or counter to it?

It does not help to know, with an intuitive glow, that you will be happier with less stuff to move around if, at that moment, you are ordering more stuff from a catalog. Habits of reassurance are hard to break and hard to replace with new habits of internal safety. The more powerful and personal your vision, the more it demands of you.

This is a time when it helps to lay out a treasure map. Put the dream or goal at one end of a road, and yourself at the other. Try to imagine the barriers that are in your way, or record them as they occur. Awareness is everything. A visual diary of the pitfalls in your personality helps.

Most of us carry old beliefs, responses, and fears that will surface over and over as barriers to change. I have learned to treat them as visitors. I joke with them, "I remember you," and then I leave them behind.

How does what you now know and want fit in with the life you are living? Can you follow it and still meet your responsibilities to your family and community? Wisdom is meant to enhance your life and the life of your community. The answers to your questions are not considered to be true, in any wisdom tradition, if they do not also serve the good of the community. The answers must have meaning beyond your own ego needs.

CHECKING THE FIT

If you need to leave your job or you want more freedom to be creative, it does not mean that you can abandon your children or commitments. Checking the fit means literally seeing how you can hold on to your new knowledge, change your life, and still follow your highest values. If you need to leave people, you must participate in a gentle and ethical process of change.

You will probably have to take some risks as you make changes. You will confront some people in your life when you try to clear out the past. You will look at your house, work, community, service, politics, and religion in different ways. You will start thinking about groups or individuals who would offer support for the changes you want to make. There are many personal support groups, as well as people, working to solve problems of violence, poverty, abuse of children, destruction of the environment, and virtually any world issue that touches your heart.

You seek wisdom alone, but you can turn to your community and your friends for help in making your life and our world what you believe it can be.

Making the Commitment

Until one is committed, there is hesitancy, the chance to draw back, always ineffectiveness, concerning all acts of initiative and creation. The moment one definitely commits oneself, then Providence moves too.

—J. W. Von Goethe

ONCE SOME OF the answers are yours, and they seem to fit, the next step is acting on them. Try to formulate some plans or, at least, a step in the direction in which you wish to go. You will begin withdrawing now from the vulnerability you felt in some of the other steps. You may feel ambivalent about how to put the knowledge directly into your life.

Remember that the wisdom process puts you in a vulnerable state because you have laid aside some of your routine defenses. When you slow yourself down and open up, it takes a while to restore your defenses and filters.

When you are ready to return home, if you have taken a physical as well as a spiritual journey, keep this in mind. Try to reenter your work and activities at a slow pace. You will be preoccupied, vague, ambivalent. Note how you feel, and don't push yourself. You may feel you are in neutral, but changes are taking place within. Try to avoid situations or people who will draw energy away from you.

Review the schedule you carry each week, review the things you do, review the wedges of your life again, and write down at least one change you are willing to commit to. In my case, it was obvious: Take steps to reduce the possibility of further abandonment, and strengthen my belief that I could create safety for myself. That meant giving up a relationship I had been struggling with, and choosing friends with greater care.

Keep your wisdom experiences to yourself until they have become a more stable part of your being.

Others will sense the change in you, the increased power, and it will make some people uncomfortable. Spend your time with people who offer support and acceptance. Our culture is still intolerant of alternative paths to knowledge.

Give yourself time to check the fit, again, of the information you have received before announcing specific changes or involving others. Review your plans and your commitment. Small steps toward your goal are much more likely to be successful, at first, than large ones. Small steps build confidence and add up sooner or later to a transformation.

People who are willing to be humble and vulnerable, who take the wisdom process seriously, have an extraordinary opportunity to become achievers and leaders. They have the insight and the strength to create change in ways that were once thought to be impossible.

STEP TWENTY

Transformation

After a time of decay comes the turning point. The power-
ful light that has been banished returns. There is move-
ment, but it is not brought about by force... The movement
is natural, arising spontaneously. For this reason the trans-
formation of the old becomes easy. The old is discarded, and
the new is introduced. Both measures accord with time;
therefore no harm results.

—I Ching

THE LAST STEP of a vision journey is a paradigm
shift. The information you receive on your journey can
be so clear and so powerful that it creates a new per-
spective and, therefore, alters every part of your life.
There is a moment of synthesis and integration when
your values become clear.

"Paradigm shift" is a concept first used by Thomas Kuhn in *The Structure of Scientific Revolutions*. It refers to a change in the fundamental rules, the model we use to understand.

Transformation takes place when your entire way of thought about a problem is altered: "Oh my God, it was my problem, not theirs!" The genius of this transformation is that it produces a kind of magic. You are able to synthesize out of all the emotions, images, signals, forecasts, and alternatives, a clear vision of the future. It is simple, easily understood, clearly desirable, and energizing.

The experience of transformation is permanent. In the case of my abandonment, I no longer have the feelings of fear. When painful things happen, I can quickly get past them. I can lean into the pain instead of away from it. I can move through it. It is as if the old memories have been replaced, the imprint is gone. I can pick up my old fears in others and treat them as I would have wished to be treated.

A transformation does not lead to perfection.

There will always be changes and missteps. It does create a clarity about what you want and your commitment to it.

How much a part of your daily life and thought has the information you received on your journey become? Has it changed the way you treat yourself? Has it changed the way you treat others? Do you have moments of feeling like a citizen of the world? Do you feel more connected to life?

The wisdom journey is a process of recognizing what is true. Transformation is the feeling of it becoming an integral part of your character. Your life begins to reflect the work you have done and the commitment you have made.

In my own life, years ago, I did one of the exercises in step two. I imagined two people talking about me around the corner at the medical school where I was teaching. What did I want to overhear them saying? I cared too much about what others thought of me. I imagined they would say, She's smart, she will be a full professor. Instead, what I heard when I asked the question in a wisdom environment was, "She cares." It was a thought that changed my life. I began to be much more involved in my community and eventually left the university.

One evening five years later I was introduced as a speaker at a banquet. The person introducing me went through the usual list of credits and ended by gesturing toward me and saying, "She is a woman who cares." I began to cry because what I was and what I wanted to be were becoming one. It was one of the supreme moments of my life.

When I faced a painful divorce some years later, I repeated the exercise. This time I heard them saying, "She's decent." I thought that was pretty useless until I realized that perhaps all I could hold on to in this sad time were my ethics. I realized that long after I had been healed from the loss of love, I would have to face how I had behaved.

I asked the question again, two years later, when I was recovering from the divorce. The disembodied voices around the corner said with a chuckle, "She's still trying to figure it out." They were right.

The last time I used this exercise I received the most powerful of responses. The voices whispered, "She is learning to love."

As I completed this book I took the time to go through the exercise again and the message startled me. "She doesn't care." What does that mean? I'm still a caring person. Then I began to understand how true the statement is. I rarely need to know what others think of me anymore. I am almost through that struggle. I know there are others ahead.

It is a heroic act to make even the smallest change that contributes to the life of this world. You have begun to take steps toward enlightenment if you are willing to stretch your allegiances beyond your culture and toward the world. There is no vision more powerful than the one that links you to all of life.

Wisdom is the long process of learning to be kind. You will find no love that rewards more consistently or deeply than the love one has for the world. Slow down, breathe deeply, let go, follow your heart, and the universe will move.

BIBLIOGRAPHY

Bloch, Douglas. *Listening to Your Inner Voice*. Indianapolis: CompCare Publishers, 1991.

Bly, Robert and William Booth, ed. *A Little Book on the Human Shadow*. San Francisco: Harper & Row, 1988.

Campbell, Joseph. *The Hero With a Thousand Faces*. New Jersey: Princeton University Press, 1972.

Campbell, Joseph. *The Power of Myth*. New York: Doubleday, 1988.

Csikzentmihalyi, Mihaly. *Flow*. New York: Harper Collins, 1991.

Eliade, Mircea. *Rites and Symbols of Initiation*. New York: Harper & Row, 1975.

Gendlin, Eugene T. *Focusing*. New York: Bantam Books, 1981.

Halifax, Joan. *Shamanic Voices*. New York: E.P. Dutton, 1979.

Hanh, Thich Nhat. *The Miracle of Mindfulness!: A Manual of Mediation*. Boston: Beacon Press, 1976.

Hoffer, Eric. *The Temper of Our Times*. New York: Harper Collins, 1967.

Kingston, Maxine Hong. *The Tripmaster Monkey*. New York: Knopf, 1990.

Kuhn, Thomas S. *The Structure of Scientific Revolutions*. University of Chicago Press, 1970.

Miller, Alice. *Prisoners of Childhood*. English translation. New York: Basic Books, 1981.

Moris, Alene. *Uncommon Sense*. Reston, VA: Reston Publishing Company, Inc., 1982.

Pearson, Carol. *The Hero Within*. San Francisco: Harper & Row, 1986.

Smith, Lillian. *The Journey*. New York: Norton, 1954.

Bibliography

Underhill, Evelyn. *Mysticism*. New York: Dutton, 1961.

Woodman, Marion. *The Pregnant Virgin*. Toronto: Inner City Books, 1985.

ABOUT THE AUTHOR

JENNIFER JAMES, PH.D., is a cultural anthropologist who has spent her life trying to understand how our belief systems either enhance or limit our lives. She has bridged many cultures: born in London, an immigrant from Wales as a small child, raised by an Episcopalian mother and a Baptist father on a farm in eastern Washington. She now lives by Puget Sound, just south of Seattle.

Dr. James has published books on quality of life *(Success Is the Quality of Your Journey)*, perception *(Windows)*, choice and change *(Life Is a Game of Choice)*, criticism *(Defending Yourself Against Criticism: The Slug Manual)*, understanding the good and the bad in life *(Women and the Blues)*, and cultural intelligence *(Thinking in the Future Tense)*.

She has hosted two PBS television specials, "Thinking in the Future Tense" and "A Workout for the Mind." She writes a weekly newspaper column and an Internet column.